Little Voice

A Royal Shakespeare Company Pro

Roald Dahl's

Matilda

THE MUSICAL

Music & Lyrics by Tim Minchin

First performance at The Courtyard Theatre,
Stratford-upon-Avon, 9 November 2010

First performance at The Cambridge Theatre,
London, 25 October 2011

First performance at The Shubert Theatre,
New York, 4 March 2013

With thanks to Tim Minchin, Chris Nightingale,
Caroline Chignell and Kevin Wright.

NOVELLO PUBLISHING LIMITED
part of The Music Sales Group
London / New York / Paris / Sydney / Copenhagen / Berlin / Madrid / Tokyo

Published by
Novello Publishing Limited
14-15 Berners Street, London, W1T 3LJ, UK.

Exclusive distributors:
Music Sales Limited
Distribution Centre, Newmarket Road, Bury St Edmunds, Suffolk, IP33 3YB, UK.

Music Sales Pty Limited
Units 3-4, 17 Willfox Street, Condell Park, NSW 2200, Australia.

Order No. NOV163636 ISBN 978-1-78305-105-2
This book © Copyright 2013 Novello & Company Limited.

Edited by Ruth Power.
Music arranged by Simon Foxley.
Music processed by Paul Ewers Music Design.
Piano accompaniment by Paul Knight.
Vocals by Rachel Lindley, Sinead O'Kelly and Lucy Potterton.
Engineered, mixed and mastered by Jonas Persson.
Photographs courtesy of the original London cast at
The Cambridge Theatre by Manuel Harlan. © Royal Shakespeare Company.
Cover image artwork and design by aka.

Printed in the EU.

www.musicsales.com

Naughty

Words & Music by Tim Minchin

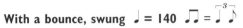

Jack and Jill... ...to
...went up the hill...

fetch a pail of wa - ter... The sub - se - quent fall...
...so they say. ...was in -

They nev-er stood a chance.

-ev - i - ta - ble.   They were writ-ten that   way.

Cm(add9)/E♭

In - no - cent vic - tims   of their sto - ry.   Like

In - no - cent vic - tims   of their sto - ry.   Like

G   D   C

Ro - me - o and Ju – li – et, 'twas writ-ten in the stars be-fore they e - ven met

Ro - me - o and Ju – li – et, 'twas writ-ten in the stars be-fore they e - ven met

that love and fate and a touch of stu - pid – i – ty would

that love and fate and a touch of stu - pid – i – ty would

rob them of their hope of liv-ing hap-pi-ly. The end-ings are of-ten a

rob them of their hope of liv-ing hap-pi-ly. The end-ings are of-ten a

Cm(add9)/Eb

G

lit-tle bit gor - y.

(Finger snaps)

I won-der why they did-n't just

lit-tle bit gor - y.

(Finger snaps)

I won-der why they did-n't just

D

C

G

7

change their sto - ry. We're told we have to do what we're told but sure-

change their sto - ry. We're told we have to do what we're told but sure-

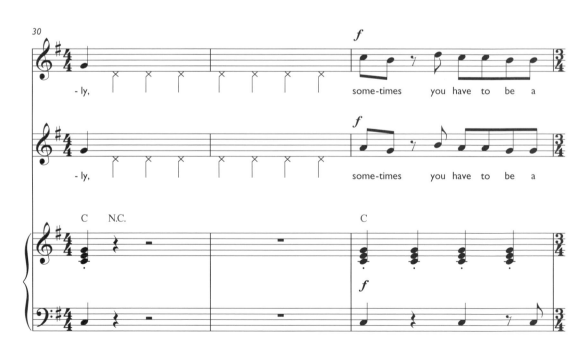

- ly, some-times you have to be a

- ly, some-times you have to be a

lit - tle bit naugh - ty.

Just be - cause you find that life's___

lit - tle bit naugh - ty.

Just be -

___ not fair,___ it___ does-n't mean that you just have to grin and bear___ it.___

- cause life's not fair, you don't have to

If you al-ways take it on the chin and wear it, noth-ing will change.

take it on the chin and wear it,

Am   G

E - ven if you're lit - tle,

noth - ing will change. E - ven if you're lit-tle you can do a lot,___ you___

C(add9)

don't let it stop you. Don't let them

must-n't let a lit-tle thing like lit - tle stop__ you.__ If you sit a - round and let them

G/B   Am

get on top,__ you might as well be say - ing you think that it's o - kay, and

get on top,__ you might as well be say - ing you think that it's o - kay, and

D⁶   B⁷/D♯   N.C.

that's   not   right!   And if it's   not___ right,

that's   not   right!   And if it's   not___ right,

B   B/D#   Em   D   Cmaj7   C   D/F#   G

you have to put it___   right.   But

you have to put it___   right.   But

Em   F#7   B7

13

School Song

Words & Music by Tim Minchin

ended, be-fore my hap-py days were o - ver, be-fore I first heard the

ended, be-fore my hap-py days were o - ver, be-fore I first heard the

peal-ing of the bell. Like you, I was cu - ri-ous, so in-no-cent I

peal-ing of the bell. Like you, I was cu - ri-ous, so in-no-cent I

asked a thou-sand ques-tions. But, un-less you want to suf-fer, lis-ten up and I will

asked a thou-sand ques-tions. But, un-less you want to suf-fer, lis-ten up and I will

teach you a thing or two. You lis-ten here, my dear, you'll be pun-ished so se-

teach you a thing or two. You lis-ten here, my dear, you'll be pun-ished so se-

18

-vere-ly if you step out of line. And if you cry it will be dou-ble. You should stay out of trou-ble and re-mem-ber to be

-vere-ly if you step out of line. And if you cry it will be dou-ble. You should stay out of trou-ble and re-mem-ber to be

ex-treme-ly care-ful.   And so you think you're

ex-treme-ly care-ful.   And so you think you're

A, B, C, D, E, F, G, H, I, J, K, L, M, N, O, P, Q, R, S, T, U, V, W,— X.

A, B, C, D, E, F, G, H, I, J, K, L, M, N, O, P, Q, R, S, T, U, V, W,— X.

Why, why, why, why, why, why, why?— Why? Just you wait for Phys-Ed!

Why, why, why, why, why, why, why?— Why? Just you wait for Phys-Ed!

When I Grow Up

Words & Music by Tim Minchin

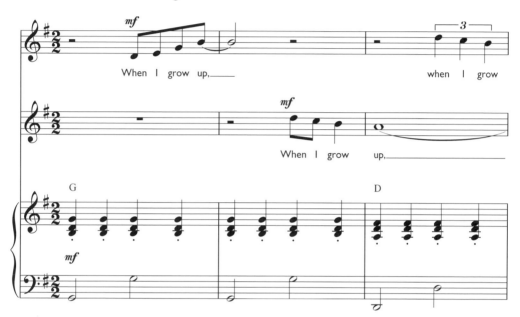

heav - y things___ you have___ to haul___ a - round with you___ when

heav - y things___ you have___ to haul___ a - round with you___ when

you're a grown up.___

you're a grown up.___

When I grow up,_____

And when I grow up,_____ when I grow

_____ I will be brave e - nough__ to fight_____ the crea - tures

up, I will be brave e - nough__ to fight_____ the crea - tures

23

that you have to fight_____ be - neath_____ the bed each night to

that you have to fight_____ be - neath_____ the bed each night to

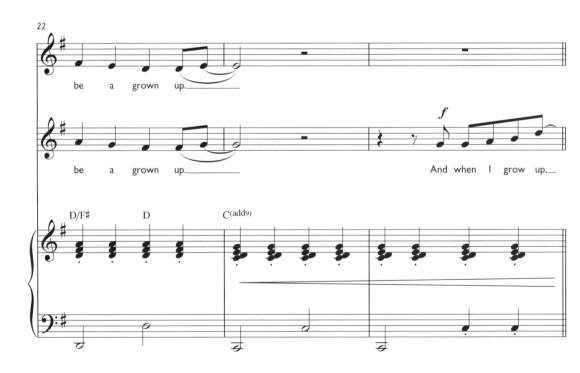

be a grown up._____

be a grown up._____ And when I grow up,_____

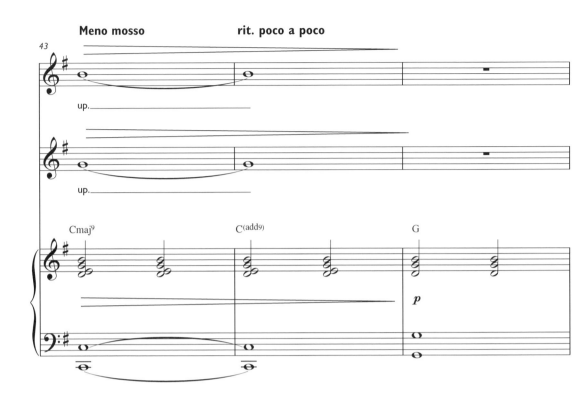

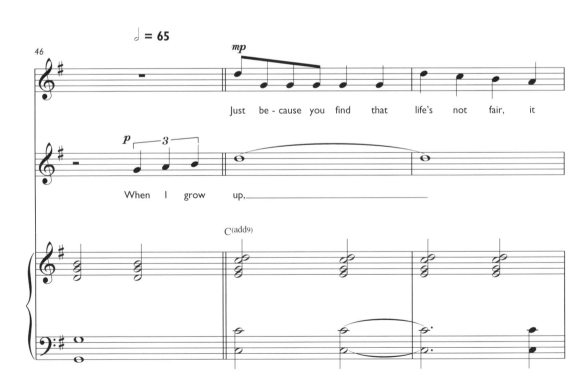

doesn't mean that you just have to grin and bear___ it. If you al-ways take it on the

when   I   grow

G/B

Am⁷

chin and wear it nothing will change. When I grow

up,   nothing will change.

G

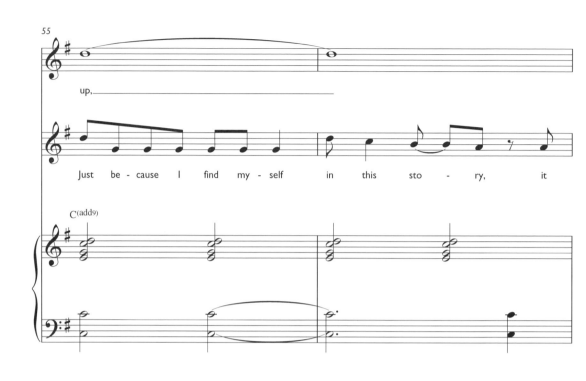

up, I might as well be say - ing I

fixed al - read - y, I might as well be say - ing I

think that it's O. K. And that's not right!

think that it's O. K. And that's not right!

My House

Words & Music by Tim Minchin

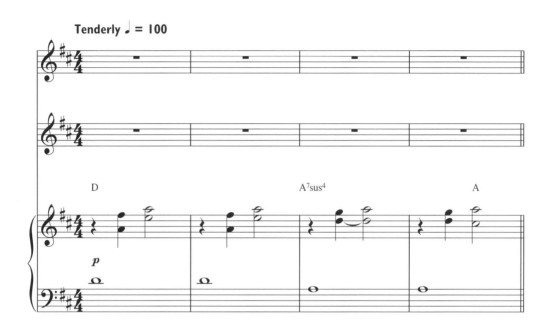

By this lamp I can read, and watch the sea - sons change.

and

I, I am_ set free! And when it's cold out -

I, I am_ set free! And when it's cold out -

- side, I feel no fear, e - ven___ in the win - ter

- side, I feel no fear, e - ven___ in the win - ter

A/C♯   A

storms. I am warmed by a small but stub - born fire___

storms. I am warmed by a small but stub - born fire___

Bm   F♯m   G

and there is no-where I would rath-er

and there is no-where I would rath-er

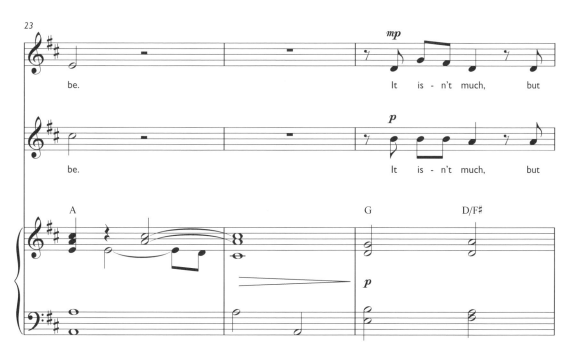

be. It is-n't much, but

be. It is-n't much, but

it is___ e - nough   for   me.

it is___ e - nough   for   me.

It is - n't much, but   it   is___ e - nough   for   me.

It is - n't much, but   it   is___ e - nough   for   me.

rit. poco a poco

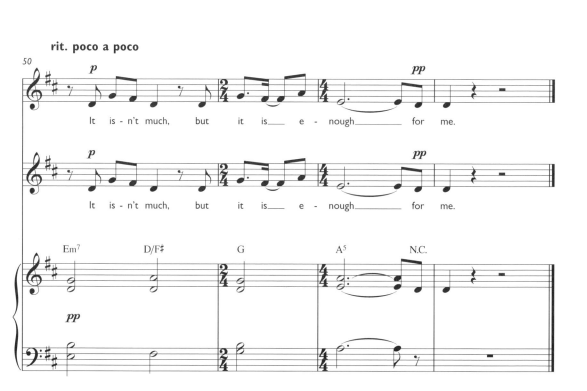

Revolting Children

Words & Music by Tim Minchin

re - volt - ing songs us - ing_____ re - volt - ing rhymes. We'll be_____

re - volt - ing songs us - ing_____ re - volt - ing rhymes. We'll be_____

re - volt - ing chil - dren till our re - volt - ing's done and we'll

re - volt - ing chil - dren till our re - volt - ing's done and we'll

41

43

line. But if we dis-o-bey at the same time, there is noth-ing that the Trunch-bull can

line. But if we dis-o-bey at the same time, there is noth-ing that the Trunch-bull can

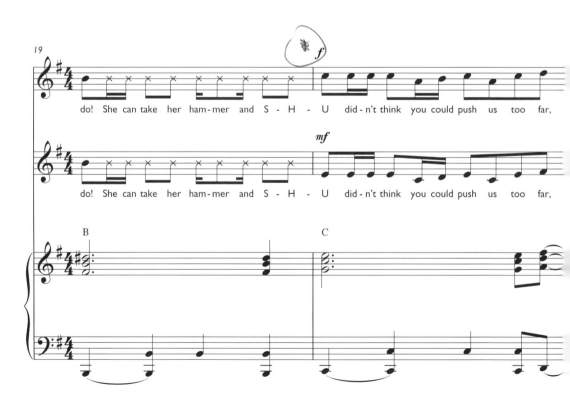

do! She can take her ham-mer and S - H - U - did-n't think you could push us too far,

do! She can take her ham-mer and S - H - U - did-n't think you could push us too far,

re-volt-ing rhymes. We'll be___ re-volt-ing child-ren till our re-volt-ing's done. It is

re-volt-ing rhymes. We'll be___ re-volt-ing child-ren till our re-volt-ing's done. It is

2 - L - 8 - 4 - U! We are___ 2 - L - 8 - 4 - U E - R - E - volt-ing!

2 - L - 8 - 4 - U! We are___ 2 - L - 8 - 4 - U E - R - E - volt-ing!

47

Track Listing

1. Naughty (from 'Matilda The Musical')
(Minchin)
Kobalt Music Publishing Limited
Full Performance

2. School Song (from 'Matilda The Musical')
(Minchin)
Kobalt Music Publishing Limited
Full Performance

3. When I Grow Up (from 'Matilda The Musical')
(Minchin)
Kobalt Music Publishing Limited
Full Performance

4. My House (from 'Matilda The Musical')
(Minchin)
Kobalt Music Publishing Limited
Full Performance

5. Revolting Children (from 'Matilda The Musical')
(Minchin)
Kobalt Music Publishing Limited
Full Performance

6. Naughty (from 'Matilda The Musical')
(Minchin)
Kobalt Music Publishing Limited
Piano Accompaniment

7. School Song (from 'Matilda The Musical')
(Minchin)
Kobalt Music Publishing Limited
Piano Accompaniment

8. When I Grow Up (from 'Matilda The Musical')
(Minchin)
Kobalt Music Publishing Limited
Piano Accompaniment

9. My House (from 'Matilda The Musical')
(Minchin)
Kobalt Music Publishing Limited
Piano Accompaniment

10. Revolting Children (from 'Matilda The Musical')
(Minchin)
Kobalt Music Publishing Limited
Piano Accompaniment